HOW TO RAISE
a Billionaire Genius

HOW TO RAISE
a Billionaire Genius

GUARANTEE YOUR CRYING POOP MONSTER
GROWS UP TO BE BETTER THAN ALL THE OTHER KIDS

Sean Campbell and D. Hornby

illustrations by Valentin Ramon

Ulysses Press

Published by:
Ulysses Press
P.O. Box 3440
Berkeley, CA 94703
www.ulyssespress.com

ISBN: 978-1-61243-120-8
Library of Congress Catalog Number 2012951891

Printed in China by Everbest through Four Colour Print Group

10 9 8 7 6 5 4 3 2 1

Acquisitions Editor: Kelly Reed
Managing Editor: Claire Chun
Editor: Jessica Benner
Proofreader: Elyce Berrigan-Dunlop
Interior design and layout: Rebecca Lown
Cover design: what!design @ whatweb.com
Cover illustrations: © Valentin Ramon

PLEASE NOTE: *How to Raise a Billionaire Genius* is a work of parody in
book format. No affiliation with, and no sponsorship
or endorsement by, the celebrities or products that are
mentioned in this work is claimed or suggested.

For the Kids

Contents

How to Raise a Billionaire

WHAT'S A MILLIONAIRE GOING TO DO?
BUY YOU HALF A HOUSE?

MONEY CAN BUY HAPPINESS.

THERE, I SAID IT.

IF ANYONE SAYS OTHERWISE,

TEACH YOUR FUTURE

WEALTHY DAUGHTER TO SLAP THAT LIE

OUT OF THEIR MOUTH WITH HER

LOUIS VUITTON HANDBAG.

Conception

Just have sex on a bed of money. All that cash on hand will drive your greedy sperm into a frenzy. Your middle-class sperm might come on strong at the start, but eventually they'll start to doubt whether all that risk and hard work are really worth it and will settle down in a less expensive area— like the fallopian tubes—to work off their car payments.

In the Womb

Inspire your womb tycoon with the noise of the stock market. Loud bells, profanity, and yelling on the trading floor are like poetry to a little billionaire's ears.

Early Years

Like Pavlov's dogs, you need to train your child to salivate
at the smell of money. Burn a bit of a dollar bill on
a regular basis. When he asks what that smell is,
jam a piece of cake in his mouth.

Choosing an Industry

If your child shows an aptitude for exploiting the
environment, you might want to consider the oil industry.
You just hire some guys to suck old dinosaurs out of the
ground through long straws and—bada-boom!—you're rich.

If human exploitation is more her thing, sweatshops in
South Cheapsland are the way to go. Build products out
of lead and asbestos to sell to Americans who never realized
they needed such a thing until they saw the
"50 percent off" sign. Simple. Effective. Billionaire.

Education

Bill Gates, Steve Jobs, and Oprah Winfrey all dropped out of college. Which should tell you that while the first few semesters make you a billionaire; the final years negate all that early promise. Your child's sophomore year should be all about driving over a flaming pile of his old textbooks in his Maserati.

Toys

Your child gets one toy: Monopoly. If she's not rushing around town tearing down her own houses to build hotels while throwing friends in jail for not paying their rent, all while driving a brand-new oversized Lexus Thimble, then you have failed as a parent.

BILLIONAIRE

Appropriate Names

FOR A GIRL:

Mrs. Dr. Howard Buckingham

Lady Duchess of Diamondton

FOR A BOY:

Dieter Von Mansionhouse

King or Prince *any hotel chain*

(as in King Marriott or Prince Best Western)

How to Raise a Genius

E = MCEASYLIFE.

IMAGINE A FUTURE IN WHICH YOU
ARE SURROUNDED BY THE PIERCING
RED EYES OF A DOZEN MENACING ROBOTS.
ONE OF THEM HANDS YOU A COLD BEER.
ANOTHER RUBS YOUR SHOULDERS WHILE
MICROWAVING POPCORN IN ITS ROBO-
TORSO. YOUR GENIUS CHILD STANDS
BEHIND THEM WITH A REMOTE CONTROL,
PROUDLY SHOWING OFF THE
FEATURES OF HER ENTRY TO
THE GRADE 3 SCIENCE FAIR.

Conception

It's pretty controversial, but you and your partner
must have sex ... *mathematically*.

That's right, it's time to get out your graphing
calculator and get busy. If you really want to freak it,
reach for that abacus. Oh ... yeah ... that's the right spot.
And you know it's the right spot because you found it
using Pythagoras's theorem.

Diet

The only guaranteed brain food is brains themselves. On
our playfully titled "zombie diet," your genius child will
ingest such delicious meals as "limbic pasta," "garlic-roasted
cerebellum," and "the gray matter platter."
They all look and taste like pablum.

Clothing

Dress your genius in a corduroy blazer at all times, keeping in mind the need to reinforce the elbows with extra material. Geniuses have uncommonly sharp elbows.

Early Training

To ensure that all your child's nutrition is focused directly on his massive brain, you need to discourage the use of the much less useful "arms" and "legs." An electric wheelchair with a breath control system should fit your needs nicely. Massage your kid's brain twice daily with fish oil to encourage growth while discouraging IQ-draining "friends."

When to Give Up

You should be able to spot the genius in your baby pretty much right from birth. If your baby drools or makes a lot of dumb-sounding noises, it's probably a lost cause. Consider the chapters on professional athlete or president as fallback options.

Appropriate Names

FOR A GIRL:
Madame Curie Us
Gain an extra 5 IQ points for every additional middle initial

FOR A BOY:
Egon
Leonardo
Really any of the Ninja Turtles will do

How to Raise a Pope

JESUS WILL TRULY BE YOUR HOMEBOY.

ENVISION YOUR FUTURE FAMILY
REUNIONS WITH THE HOLY BISHOP
OF ROME WORKING THE BARBECUE.
FROM THE SMOKE WAFTING IN YOUR
DIRECTION, YOU KNOW THOSE BABY
BACK RIBS HAVE JUST THE RIGHT
AMOUNT OF FRANKINCENSE.
BREATHE DEEP. THE AIR IS RICH
WITH GRADE A PORK PRODUCT,
ANCIENT ARABIAN SPICES, AND
ETERNAL SALVATION.

Conception

There's one strategy that stands out above the rest to increase your odds of conceiving a future pope: sleep with the acting pope. This will be extremely difficult, as your target is celibate, old, and gross.

First, get close to him in a crowd. When you go to kiss his ring, just go ahead and get his whole finger in your mouth. Start really working that finger, while confessing your sexiest sins rapid fire.

In the Womb

As far as prenatal music goes, it's going to have to be organ music. If you don't know how to play, it's not a big deal. I mean, would anyone, let alone your fetus, really notice? Just go heavy on a few keys. Nice and slow. There, now you know how to play the organ.

Delivery

As soon as that baby touches your vagina, he has sinned. The best way to limit the damage to his reputation is to have him absolved as quickly as possible. For this reason, you should give birth in a confessional.

When to Give Up

If your child is non-Italian, your odds are much reduced, but you still have a chance. If your child is not white … well, good luck.

For Girls

Women and the church sort of got off on the wrong foot when Eve RUINED EVERYTHING FOR EVERYONE FOREVER. Ladies, to get back in God's good graces, I'd lobby the New Testament God. The Old Testament God? He might just tell you to get back in the kitchen.

Appropriate Names

John
Paul
John Paul

Appropriate Middle Names

XIIII
IV
XIVII

How to Raise Your Child Gay

UPGRADE YOUR AVERAGE CHILD TO FAB-U-LOUS!

GAY IS THE NEW HAPPY, WHICH,

COINCIDENTALLY, IS THE OLD GAY.

GAY PEOPLE ALL OVER THE WORLD ARE

ENJOYING BETTER PARTIES, BETTER SEX,

AND BETTER HAIRCUTS THAN THEIR

HETEROSEXUAL COUNTERPARTS.

EMPOWER YOUR CHILD TO WALK

THE PATHS THAT HETEROSEXUALS

FEAR TO TREAD.

GAY. IS. THE FUTURE.

Conception

Convincing a homosexual to breed with you is going to be tricky. Because this person is gay. You'll just have to settle for acting as gay as possible while engaging in heterosexual intercourse. Replace your normal sexy talk with "Eww, gross! Your junk is disgusting! Please let it end!" While this is hard on your partner's ego, your child's gay future is worth it.

In the Womb

You did it! You've got an absolutely fierce bun in the oven. Now the fun begins, because you get to start enjoying a gay lifestyle yourself—a strong parental example to your super-scrumptious little fetus. All your dreams are coming true! For your child, I mean.

The Accent

Do gay people speak this way because they are gay, or are they gay because they speak this way? You can't take the chance. Children are essentially just bald, beakless parrots; start teaching your child gayspeak from day one. "Ultra fab!" "Spark-tacular!" and "LOLZ": the umbilical cutting is all these things! And that's not just a Jolly Jumper ... well, yeah, that can still be a Jolly Jumper.

Diet

The nutrients required to raise a gay son are found almost exclusively in foods of the phallic group. Cucumbers, popsicles, hot dogs without a bun. For dessert, a frozen banana standing erect in a whipped cream base garnished with two strawberries. I'm salivating.

Youth

The day comes in every child's life when they need to have that special talk about the birds and the birds. Lovingly explain the ins and outs of homosexual sex. If your child asks you to explain how sex works between a man and woman, just get a really weird look on your face and act like it's something you had never considered before.

Gay Nursery Rhymes

Use this children's classic to turn your child's future rainbow bright!

HOT CROSS BUNS!
HOT CROSS BUNS!
ONE A PENNY, TWO A PENNY, HOT CROSS BUNS!

HOT CROSS BUNS!
HOT CROSS BUNS!
IF YOU HAVE NO DAUGHTERS, GIVE THEM TO YOUR SONS!

I dare you to not be attracted to the smooth curve of a man's powerful buns after reciting that mouth-watering rhyme throughout your childhood. It just screams that hot buns are cheap son-pleasers.

Appropriate Names

FOR A GIRL:

Butch Cassidy (you can always fall back
on plain Cassidy if it doesn't work out)
Boy George (sends a pretty clear message)

FOR A BOY:

Ernie

Bert

Anything ending in "smurf"

How to Raise an Olympic Athlete

REALIZE ALL THE LIFE REWARDS OF A TANDEM DIVER.

ARE YOU THE TYPE OF PARENT
WHO BELIEVES IN DISCIPLINE
AND ATHLETICISM, BUT NOT SO MUCH
IN THE FAME, EXCESS, AND SCANDAL
ASSOCIATED WITH OUR PROFESSIONAL
ATHLETES? DO YOU WANT YOUR CHILD
TO DO WELL IN LIFE, BUT NOT
TOO WELL? THEN FORGET
MAINSTREAM SPORTS AND TURN
INSTEAD TO THE SILVER MEDAL
OF ATHLETIC CAREER PATHS:
THE OLYMPICS!

Conception

The Chinese Olympic program begins cultivating athletes at the age of four. This flagrant lack of planning is precisely why their athletes will never stand a chance against yours. A true champion should be cultivated right from the moment of conception.

To conceive a champion swimmer, consider making love to your partner from opposite ends of an Olympic-sized swimming pool. The Michael Phelps sperm only swam a few pathetic inches at conception. Your little champ has to go 50 meters through hostile chlorinated waters. Now throw on that sexy lingerie and a swim cap. Let's hit the pool!

The current record for the hundred-meter dash is 9.58 seconds. To conceive a sprinter, every sexual encounter should beat this time.

In the Womb

I'm no doctor, but I'm pretty sure a little in-the-womb training never did anybody any harm. People often shy away from the idea of being overly rough with a pregnant woman, but if you're looking for a boxer, a few light jabs to the baby bump will help get the kid ready for the ring. It's cool; she only told you not to "rub" her belly.

At Birth

Do *not* cut the umbilical cord. By leaving the cord intact, you are literally draining the life force from a loving mother and converting it into pure Olympic power.

If you have a daughter, the opportunity exists for you to stay together forever by training for a two-woman sport. Bobsledding. Beach volleyball. Your nutrient-rich child will be so powerful by this stage that she'll be able to handle the competition pretty much on her own, as Mom trails limply behind like a flat balloon.

Four-Year Cycles

Begin living your life in four-year cycles to create an Olympic monster whose heartrate and metabolism inexplicably spike at the precise moment of the opening ceremonies.

Example: the mobile above your baby's crib:

YEAR 1:

Calmly playing lullabies, moving so slowly
a Frenchman would beat it in a footrace.

YEAR 2:

Lullabies replaced with a few Bon Jovi
power ballads, speed slightly increased.

YEAR 3:

Power ballads replaced by "Chariots of Fire"
and "Eye of the Tiger," now spinning fast enough
to create a light breeze.

YEAR 4:

Speed metal at top volume. Spinning so fast
that your child is pinned down by a wind tunnel
that will help strengthen his core.

Specialize

To guarantee a lack of competition, choose a demonstration sport for your child. In 1900 the Paris Olympics included cannon shooting, ballooning, and pigeon racing. I'm guessing the French team did OK that year.

Infancy

The only chance your kid has of making any money is to pander shamelessly for corporate sponsors. As a responsible infant endorser, she should hold up any product to her smiling face for a quick photo op while waving like a champion to anyone around. Cereal box, toothpaste, tissue paper. Smile. Wave. Photo.

Pets

Also, the right pet can go a long way toward helping with the development of any infant athlete. It's a fact: nobody runs faster than those who are utterly terrified of a rabid hound. By giving your new dog/coach free reign, you can ensure that your child sprints absolutely everywhere and remains tense as a drawn bow at all times.

Screw Patriotism

Sure, the country of your child's birth might have funded all his equipment, years of training, coaches, and high-end human growth hormones, but he is a shoe-in for the Mexican luge team. Make the muy bueno choice to move to Cancun right before the Olympics so he can breeze through the preliminaries and stay focused on gold. Ole!

Appropriate Names

FOR A BOY:
Firstly Goldenstein
Carl Lewis Phelps
Apollo Ono (nonsensical, but the Greeks
invented it, so a shout out wouldn't hurt)

FOR A GIRL:
Goldy
Winnie
Winnie Goldy

How to Raise an Astronaut

FOR THE PARENTS WHO HOPE THEIR KIDS
WILL MOVE FAR, FAR AWAY.

"OH, WENDY, THAT'S GREAT

YOUR SON TOMMY GOT A RAISE AT

THE PAPER MILL. MY LITTLE TIMOTHY

JUST DISCOVERED A NEW PLANET WITH

AN EARTH-COMPATIBLE ATMOSPHERE.

I GUESS HE'S SORT OF THE SAVIOR OF

HUMANITY. BUT NO, REALLY,

TOMMY'S RAISE SOUNDS NICE."

ENOUGH SAID.

Conception

Conceiving in zero gravity is definitely your best option for breeding up an astro-baby. Failing that, your next best option is to fake it. Enter your bedroom in slow motion and on tiptoes as if walking on the moon. Throw in some Darth Vader–like "oooooo-paaaaas" for effect.

In the Womb

As an expectant father, you should be yelling "liftoff" and rattling the coffee table every time your partner stands up. As a mother(ship), you should inundate the womb with space themes, such as the introductory score to *2001: A Space Odyssey*, which conveniently is nine months long.

Delivery

Ah, delivery. Day 1. The first frontier. Delivery is always a lot of work for the father, and this is no exception. As the husband in this equation, it will be up to you to repeat the "one small step" line ad nauseam. For example, when the nurse says your wife is dilated, you say, "That's one small step for my wife's vagina, one giant leap for vaginakind."

It's simple and fun.

Appropriate Toys

When you give a girl a Barbie, she grows up taking women's studies at some liberal college and then goes out and gets a job, rebelling against everything Barbie stands for. So you see, you need to use a bit of reverse psychology when choosing the appropriate toy for your child. Find a toy that hates paying high taxes for government programs that are exciting but offer no tangible benefit to mankind.
You know, like He-Man.

Astronaut Training in Infancy

At this age, EVERY kid wants to be an astronaut.
Turning your infant's magical dream into an unhealthy
obsession won't be easy on either of you. Yet you must
ensure your child will feel like an utter failure
if she doesn't make it to space.

Count down to everything. If little Spaceman forgot to do
the mandatory morning hand-eye aptitude tests you left out,
then let Spaceman know it's time for a spanking in
"T-MINUS TEN … NINE … EIGHT … NEXT STOP,
THE SORE BOTTOM NEBULA!"
Hahahaha, fun for the whole family.

Adolescence

Space camp at every possible opportunity. Those few weeks a
year immersed in aviation, robotics, science, and math will
ensure the correct amount of alienation when your child
reenters teenage society. This "nerd-i-zation" will establish
a tremendous social barrier that will have little Spaceman
studying star charts on Friday and Saturday nights, well away
from any distracting earthbound parties.

Fitness Training

Make fitness fun with games like only allowing
your child to go to the bathroom at home. A quick sprint
home from a restaurant, soccer practice, or Disneyland
is tremendous for their stamina.

Diet

Straight Rocket Pops and Tang. As long as you're
following my advice on keeping your child physically fit,
then obesity shouldn't be a problem. Blood pressure and
diabetes, sure, but not physical fitness.

Constant Motivation

It's your duty as a space parent to never show more than luke-
warm praise. "A full scholarship to MIT? I was sort of hoping
for a nonacronym school." This strategy will keep your child
hungry for greatness/love. Going to the moon is often just an
astronaut's way of saying, "I hate you, Mom and Dad!"

Appropriate Names

FOR A GIRL:
Spock (just tell people it's Greek)
Spaceman (cut right to the chase)

FOR A BOY:
Buzz (middle name could be Aldrin or Lightyear)
JamesTKirk (all one name, like "JamesTKirk Stewart")
Insector (sounds awesome)

How to Raise a Conqueror

CONAN, GENGHIS, AND NAPOLEON ALL ROLLED
INTO A BIG BALL OF AWESOMENESS.

IMAGINE HOW GREAT LIFE WOULD
BE FOR THE PARENT OF A TOTALITARIAN
DICTATOR. DO YOU THINK A
MECHANIC CHARGED MAMA JONG IL
$400 FOR MISCELLANEOUS LABOR?
NO, THAT NEVER HAPPENED TO
MRS. KIM, BECAUSE SHE RAISED
HER BOY RIGHT.
AND SO CAN YOU.

Conception

In terms of the physical act of lovemaking, there is just
one rule: be on top. A great dictator is either on
top or fighting to get on top at all times, as should
you be. And your partner.

In the Womb

What does Jesus Christ have in common with
Harry Potter and Neo from *The Matrix*? They were all
preceded by prophecy. Your child tyrant is only nine months
away, so it's time to hire some homeless people to hold up
your cardboard slogans:

"KIMBERLY IN 4B IS EXPECTING!
EXPECTING EARTH'S NEW OVERLORD!"
"THE END IS NEAR! BECKY IS EIGHT AND A HALF MONTHS!"

Delivery

Legend says that Genghis Khan was born with a blood clot clenched tightly in his iron baby fist. The crushed remains of an intrauterine enemy, perhaps. It did a lot for his street cred around Mongolia. Try to dream up something similar for that first newborn photo.

Infancy

The schoolyard is the perfect training ground for any budding warmonger. It's already full of warring factions, desirable landmarks, and strategic headlands. A great lesson to learn early is the difficulty of an extended foreign campaign under trying conditions. Attempting to take over the soccer field in winter should serve nicely to pound this one home. Let your child see firsthand what happens as runny noses decimate his forces. Troops freeze and are forced to go home to put a jacket on. Dinnertime comes around before making significant progress on the outer flanks. If only Napoleon's parents had been so long sighted.

Manners

You can't say totalitarian dictator without also saying "total dick." You can skip finishing school this time; cultural refinement is not a requirement.

For Girls

Female tyrants are not always obvious. That herdswoman in the yak-hide pantsuit behind Genghis was Mrs. Khan. China fell specifically because Genghis was scared to come home otherwise. Once your daughter conquers the conqueror, he's just the lead soldier in her army.

Appropriate Names

FOR A BOY:
Killzor Maimsalot
Don Ofdoom
Bieber Khan

FOR A GIRL:
Isla Killiya
Di Peasants

How to Raise a Trophy Spouse

USE THE CHILD YOU'RE STUCK WITH TO LURE
IN THE ONE YOU REALLY WANT.

THE DEDICATED AND HARDWORKING
PARENTS READING OTHER CHAPTERS
ARE SAYING THINGS LIKE "I WANT
MY CHILD TO BE LIKE
LEONARDO DICAPRIO" OR "MAYBE
SHE COULD GROW UP TO BE
LIKE ELLEN!" BY CHOOSING THE
TROPHY ROUTE, YOU AREN'T
SETTLING FOR A CHEAP CLONE.
YOU'RE CONFIDENTLY TELLING
THE WORLD, "I WANT LEO
AND ELLEN TO BE MY CHILDREN.
IN-LAWS."

Conception

In other chapters I've been all, "You need to go out and get some good genes for your baby." "The seed you choose is all important!" Blah blah blah. Since you're just molding your whatever child to attract someone who is already amazing, you can pretty much get knocked up by anyone. In fact, maybe the dumber the better so you have a blank slate to work with when your baby is born.

Your real focus here is on quantity rather than quality. I don't want to bore you with a bunch of math here, but the more bait children you have, the better your odds of acquiring your trophy child. Pay close attention to drug commercials that say, "Pregnant women should avoid contact with Deformium!" Just go ahead and start touching all of those. That'll split your zygote like a cheese grater.

In the Womb

Being pregnant with several children is no time to rest.
Get busy and start creating mobiles that feature photos of
your target child as it chimes through a song your target child
wrote or inspired. If they haven't written or inspired a song
yet, then you're going to want to dream a bit bigger.
Seriously, not even one song? This chapter is powerful
enough to snag a Michael Buble, and you've got Channing
Tatum on the brain? For shame.

Delivery

If at all possible, have your target child deliver your bait
child. Say it's a Make-A-Wish Foundation type thing and
have them come to the hospital. If you take enough photos,
it will make a great slideshow at their wedding in twenty years.
Sixteen if you move to Kentucky.

Early Childhood

Throughout their lives, trophy people are inundated with hotness. Some might still desire it, but your kid will need some other kind of unique twist to be truly desirable. That unique twist could certainly be obsession.

A handy little technique to build obsession in their early childhood is to only celebrate your target child's birthday. Sure, some of your little bait children might question this practice at some point, and they might even cry, but then they don't get any of Ryan Gosling's birthday cake. That will teach everyone to fall in line and to love Ryan Gosling for sharing his precious birthday cake with them. What a great guy Ryan Gosling is. Don't you just want to get married to him someday?

Go Foreign

If your kid is sadly unappealing in the domestic trophy market, don't be afraid to go foreign. There's no telling how the Armenian czar of the moment likes to get his freak on.

Define and Mold

You don't need to reinvent the relationship wheel here.
You already know what your trophy child likes.
You just need to give birth to a younger, and
therefore more appealing, version of the wheel.

About 50 percent of you out there want Oprah to be your trophy child. I don't blame you; she's pretty awesome. Incredibly wealthy, compassionate, funny, and smart. Basically everything you dream for your child that they will never be. We already know what Oprah likes. She has her "favorite things" she gives away every year; she likes books and Steadman. When your bait child is born, nurture him to be compassionate, to like all of Oprah's favorite things each year, and be well read. All while cultivating one of the world's great mustaches and looking like an aerobics fitness model from the 1980s.

Since this book will easily become an international sensation, I know all you un-American wine sippers out there will want something called a David Beckham. He likes tattoos, soccer, nannies, situps, and singing divas who can't carry a tune. When your bait child is born, just bust out the Junior Miss Tattooing kit and go wild. Then give her a karaoke machine, but DO NOT give her lessons.

Appropriate Names

FOR A GIRL:
Yoko
Mrs. Trump

FOR A BOY:
Ashton
Mr. Winfrey (first name: Future)

How to Raise a Teen Mom

THE SHORTCUT TO GRANDCHILDREN.

"MY FAMILY MAKES ME THE RICHEST PERSON IN THE WORLD." YOU HEAR IT ALL THE TIME FROM DRIVERS OF '98 DODGE CARAVANS. IF YOU TOO WANT TO GET RICH "ON THE INSIDE," THERE'S ONE QUICK METHOD TO GROWING A FAMILY TREE TO RIVAL THE GREAT BARRIER REEF: RAISE YOUR CHILDREN TO BECOME TEEN PARENTS.

Conception

We're on a pretty ambitious timeline here, so go ahead and start having sex while reading this sentence. In progress? Good. Now speed things up a notch; we don't have all day. You and your partner should be gyrating at roughly the same frequency as the paint shaker at the hardware store. Done? Take a pregnancy test. Repeat.

How Many Grandchildren Will This Get Me?

Here's a conservative scenario: three children of your own, thirteen-year generation cycles, and an anticipated litter of three children per child. In just sixty-five years you will have created over 58 thousand pounds of living ancestors. Respectable even by Mormon standards.

In the Womb

A great time to kick back and study up on your instructional videos: *Teen Mom*, seasons 1 through 5.

Birth

The second your baby is born, get her a gurney next to yours in the maternity ward. Have other people's newborns swaddled and put in her arms. She'll love it.

Toys

Babies. Her babies. Until then, nothing.

Youth

If only there were some organization that would take your child in, teach them the evils of birth control, and then force them to dress in super alluring short, plaid skirts every single day of the week. Oh, but there is! It's time to enroll your daughter in Catholic school.

Where to Live

Definitely Mississippi. Mississippi has the highest rate of teen pregnancies in the United States. Maybe it's the hot weather, allowing young people to wear next to nothing. Maybe it's all the hoedowns. Or maybe it's a fervently religious community that actively discourages contraception but also does a poor job promoting abstinence. Move there.

Useful Mythology

"The rhythm method of contraception
means listening to music while you do it."
"A boy with freckles cannot get you pregnant."
"You can't get pregnant if it's your first time.
That day."
"God hates condoms."

Appropriate Names

FOR A BOY:
See Ya (or C.Ya if you want to be awesome)
Breeder

FOR A GIRL:
Mom
Mommy
Kaitlyn (all huge sluts)

How to Raise a Pop Singer

BUY MY COMPANION BOOK, *HOW TO GET YOUR CHILD THROUGH REHAB.*

POP SINGERS ARE THE MOST
WORSHIPPED FIGURES SINCE
JESUS CHRIST RELEASED HIS FIRST HIT
SINGLE AT AGE FIFTEEN. WE LOVE THEM.
WE LOVE WHEN THEY SING.
WE LOVE THE WAY THEY DRESS.
WE MIGHT OCCASIONALLY
HATE THEM WHEN THEY SHAVE
THEIR HEAD, BUT SINCE WE ALSO
LOVE TO HATE THEM,
WE'RE RIGHT BACK TO LOVE AGAIN.

Conception

Ideally, you'll want to have your child sired by a current or
near current pop icon. Honestly, the way they party, it's
probably harder to avoid having your
child fathered by Usher.

In the Womb

You are preparing your child for a life under the spotlight,
so start early and keep a spotlight focused on the womb at
all times. This might be awkward when in a movie theater or
driving at night, but this is the sacrifice you need to make for
stardom. All future sacrifices will rest on the sexy
undernourished shoulders of your star-to-be.

Delivery

Actual birth: Gross. Clean you and your baby up;
you look terrible.

Media birth (six weeks later): Watch the photographers' faces
light up with amazement as Mom leaps off the delivery room
table to land in the splits while waving her dancing newborn
in the air to the rhythm of its first hit single.
Tomorrow's headline: "A Star Is Born."

Infancy

Ensure your child's hair/nails/face are professionally done
up the moment their hair/nails/face don't swell up upon
contact with those luxuriously toxic beauty products.
The next photo op is now.

Breakups and Breakdowns

To really achieve the highest honors our media can bestow,
your child must learn how to screw up. Spectacularly.
Because in reality just watching somebody with a perfect body
make all the right moves in life starts to get tedious pretty
fast. "Oh. You're naturally talented, superhot, rich,
dating a professional athlete, and you donate half your
profits to charity? Bitch."

B E H A V I O R   T A B L E

BEHAVIOR	BENEFITS
BREAK UP WITH CELEBRITY PARTNER AFTER CHEATING	You're single and open for business.
GAIN WEIGHT	You physically take up more room on the magazine cover, making you more visible to your public.
ENSUING ANOREXIA	You look fabulous!
DRUGS/ALCOHOL	You just like to party; fans love that you're "living the dream."
MENTAL BREAKDOWN	When your publicist said it was stress induced, people felt bad for you. I mean, you were working so hard to entertain them. Them.
FIGHT WITH PAPARAZZI	Use your Grammy to break a few noses, and it will never be forgotten.

Appropriate Names

FOR A GIRL:
Britney
Xtina
Maybe just choose twenty to thirty middle names and use the
one that's hot/not taken when she starts touring

FOR A BOY:
Justin
Some kind of styled phallic symbol

How to Raise a Vampire

LET YOUR HUSBAND CHIP IN WITH
THE BREASTFEEDING.

VAMPIRES ARE IMMORTAL AND

ARE DEFINITELY SEXY AS FAR AS

ALBINO SERIAL KILLERS GO,

BUT ARE YOU SERIOUSLY READING THIS

CHAPTER? CHECK YOUR CALENDAR,

VAMPIRES WERE LAST WEEK.

COME BACK NEXT WEEK WHEN

VAMPIRES HAVE BECOME IRONIC.

Conception

There are only a few ways to actually conceive a vampire child, and none are overly enjoyable for the ladies. They're all a bit throat teary. In this rare case, I recommend starting your child molding after conception. Let your little one experience the joy of being chased and drained into the destiny you've chosen for him.

In the Womb

It stands to reason that you can turn your unborn child into a vampire by being bitten when you're preggers. You feel that? That's logic kicking your belly. However, what's not logical is taking two incisors for the team when you're already giving birth to the little ingrate. Through your groin. Again, give birth to a human, then turn her.

Birth

You'll want to turn your baby into a vampire as quickly as possible, so when you start feeling the contractions, it's time to chum the water, as it were. Keep a plastic bag of blood in your birth kit and make sure the blood is AD Rh negative, the rarest blood type. That stuff is like Dom Perignon to vampires.

Early Years

One of the most overlooked advantages of a vampire child is the complete ease of dealing with daycare during the preschool years. While your neighbor struggles to make ends meet paying high childcare costs, you just put your little angel in a box and close the lid.

What parents do when their vampire children
"play with their food" and their food
gets pregnant - pie chart

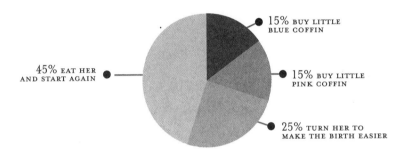

45% EAT HER
AND START AGAIN

15% BUY LITTLE
BLUE COFFIN

15% BUY LITTLE
PINK COFFIN

25% TURN HER TO
MAKE THE BIRTH EASIER

Watch Out for Vampire Hunters

Unfortunately, there will be a professional or two hunting
your child throughout her immortal life. These sad
characters didn't have a parent who loved them enough to
turn them into a vampire, and now they roam the earth
looking for the undead and Mommy's acceptance.
Beware.

Potential for Putting Neighbors in Place

Wouldn't it just be great to lean over the fence and put that stuck-up neighbor lady in her place? "Oh, your Billy came in third at the science fair?" you say. "Well, my Alicia is immortal and sexily drinks the blood of innocents. Send Billy over for a play date later. You know, when the sun goes down." Take that to your bake sale, Molly!

Education

Two words: home schooling. Although a bit more effort on the part of the parent, home schooling contributes more than anything else to the creepy social awkwardness so common in vampire kind. Just be thankful your kid wasn't home schooled and NOT a vampire. Creepy and awkward without brooding and dangerous is just …
creepy and awkward.

Good Hygiene

Be sure to teach your child the proper way to brush his teeth.
Always good advice. Now more than ever.

Appropriate Names

FOR A BOY:
Edward
Collin
Dennis
Some other wimpy English-sounding name

FOR A GIRL:
Eva
Blake
Giselle
Some other model DiCaprio has nailed

How to Raise a Superhero

HINT: RADIOACTIVE PETS.

THERE ARE MANY GREAT REASONS
FOR WANTING TO BIRTH A SUPERHERO:
REVENGE, RETRIBUTION, VENGEANCE,
REPRISAL ... IT'S DIFFERENT
FOR EVERYONE. WHATEVER THE
CASE MAY BE, PREPARING YOUR
CHILD FOR A LIFE OF IDENTITY CRISES,
GENDER CONFUSION, AND FAILED
RELATIONSHIPS CAN BRING
A GREAT SENSE OF SATISFACTION
TO THE PROUD SUPERPARENT.

Practical Applications

You'll burst with pride when your superkid saves the world from impending disaster, but how often does that come up? Once a year if you're lucky. It's the day-to-day stuff that makes a superkid great. Save on the electric bill by having your child shoot lightning bolts into the wall sockets. Save on other costs by shooting lightning bolts at them, too. There's no problem lightning can't solve when carefully aimed at somebody who knows the solution.

Conception

A romantic vacation getaway. An intimate picnic in a private glade beneath a purple sunset. A herd of graceful five-legged elk prancing across the scorched earth. If you don't conceive a hero during your vacation at Chernobyl, you can always try putting your sperm in the microwave.

In the Womb

The tanning bed is a great tool for incubating your superfetus. Not only will all that extra radiation increase her chances of mutation, but use it enough, and your little peanut will get a tawny tan. When's the last time you saw a pasty superhero?

Birth

If you're lucky, he'll just shoot right out of there, one arm raised out in front.

Childhood

Early childhood trauma is always the main ingredient in a superrecipe. As a parent, it's your duty to walk around highways with your eyes closed and bad neighborhoods with them open. Wide open, staring thugs in the face. Your constant peril will motivate and shape the rest of your child's superlife.

The Superpower of Money

Are you a billionaire who owns a multinational research and development corporation? Batman and Ironman are just fancy pseudonyms for Moneyman and Captain Spendsalot. A strong sense of morals, a kindhearted and insightful assistant, and a billion-dollar suit are a sure-fire ticket to the superpantheon.

Relationships

When your superchild hits puberty, explain to him in simple terms that he can never be with a person of the opposite sex. Because to superheroes, love is a curse that only brings danger and pain. Teenagers are pretty reasonable; he should get it.

Make Sure Your Superchild Is Super Good Looking

You'll also want to monitor your child's level of attractiveness as they develop their superpowers. Superheroes are incredibly fit and good looking. If your little rug rat has trouble seeing his targets past his giant nose and buck teeth, you might be nurturing a future evil villain. Unattractiveness is often a trait of their ilk.

Superheroine

At first it will seem like a superheroine would be a great match for your superchild. They'll share laughs over the big group of henchmen who come at them one at a time, the bad aim of local police, and mimosas after cape shopping. But beware. One day she's saving a busload of orphans hanging precariously over a cliff in Guatemala, and the next she's giving you really pissy remarks about your driving from the passenger seat. Pissy comments are just a precursor to joining your archenemy (of all people!) for an evil scheme. Who needs that headache?

SUPERHERO

Appropriate Names

FOR A GIRL:
Cat-something
Something-ess

FOR A BOY:
His last name should definitely be Man
Clark
Kent
Sebastian
(for more of the childhood trauma thing)

How to Raise a Fireman

THIS PROFESSION IS HOT! GET IT?!?!?

REMEMBER WHEN YOU HAD A GREASE
FIRE, AND YOUR POPE CHILD JUST
HUDDLED IN THE CORNER, PRAYING FOR
THE FLAMES TO STOP? OR THE TIME
YOUR CAT RAN UP THE TREE, AND
YOUR SUPERMODEL KID SCREAMED IN
FEAR UNTIL SHE PASSED OUT? YOU'RE
GOING TO WANT AT LEAST ONE FIREMAN
AROUND TO ENSURE YOUR OTHER
CHILDREN SURVIVE TO MEET
THEIR DESTINIES.

Conception

Much like the profession itself, the act of conception will begin with a great fire of passion, followed by some sweaty teamwork. It will be a powerful blast from a hose that finally gets things back under control.

In the Womb

You can bet your great grandma was putting back cartons of menthols to ease her morning sickness, and she gave birth to the "greatest generation." Obviously smoking during pregnancy isn't that bad, so now is the time to spark up and get your little fireman fetus ready to brave the backdraft.

Delivery

Throughout your labor, make regular use of the fireman's pole, and really absorb the impact at the bottom with your thighs and buttocks. This is great training for your future fireman and makes delivery a snap.

Diet

Smoked salmon, smoked baby back ribs, smoked peas, smoked carrots, smoked PB and J, smoked pablum.

Training

Maybe your little guy is busy watering a particularly yellow patch of grass when ... think fast ... a Molotov cocktail hits the azaleas. As the flames are flying everywhere, make it clear that every flower that doesn't make it through this ordeal will come out of his allowance.

Bedtime

When you start to feel those eyes drooping, just shut off the
TV and announce to your fire child, "Time for bed."
Then go limp and have her carry you to your room.
Fifteen flights up.

Appropriate Names

FOR A BOY:
Blaze
Smokey the Beefcake

FOR A GIRL:
Giselle Firebrand (in my dreams)

How to Raise a President of the United States of America

HAVE YOUR CHOICE OF DOG CRITIQUED AD NAUSEAM.

THE POSSIBILITIES FOR THE ABUSE
OF POWER ARE ENDLESS WHEN YOU
GIVE BIRTH TO THE MOST
POWERFUL PERSON IN THE WORLD.
WINTER WEATHER GOT YOU DOWN?
NOTHING A CIA-ORGANIZED
TACTICAL ASSAULT ON THAT
UNFRIENDLY, SUN-SOAKED LITTLE
NATION WON'T CURE. IN YOUR NEW
POSITION AS AMBASSADOR TO THIS
NEW AMERICAN COLONY, RECENTLY
RENAMED "DADISTAN," YOU'LL HAVE
PLENTY OF BEACH TIME TO BEAT
THOSE WINTER BLUES.

Conception

Given their recent political dominance, the best place to have sex is in a Bush family bed. Preferably with a member of the Bush family. Think about it. Grandpa won't just be spoiling his favorite grandchild with Werther's Originals, he'll be bringing top secret incriminating photos of political rivals.

In the Womb

As the first vehicle in which our future president will ever travel, your uterus is now officially Womb Force One. You'll need to reinforce the walls of the presidential uterus with a combination of Kevlar sheeting and ballistic steel. If it's not too uncomfortable, station a few beefy Secret Servicemen in there as well.

Delivery

Having a state-of-the-baby address once your child has been burped and wrapped in the American flag is crucial. Get the media relationship off on the right foot. Yes, of course we drove an American-made automobile to the hospital. No, our baby has never used any recreational drugs. His position on the poor? He wants to help them. To help themselves.

Birthday Gifts

Be careful. Legos will lead your child to the life of a lowly engineer, and Dora reinforces an unhealthily positive attitude toward Mexico. You need to go uberpatriotic with those first few gifts. Watch your child's eyes light up when she unwraps a one-sixth-size replica of the Declaration of Independence. I'm sure most of those tears are tears of joy.

Attire

It will probably be a good idea to get a hard hat for your child to wear in the company of blue-collar Americans. Let your child know that he is just like them, from the eyebrows up.

Appropriate Names

FOR A GIRL:
Hillary Bush
Hillary Kennedy

FOR A BOY:
George Washington Bush Lincoln
Abraham Kennedy
George WashingtonDC

How to Raise a Supermodel

WHEN HAS ANYONE EVER LOVED A BABY
FOR ITS PERSONALITY?

THE MOST IMPORTANT THING YOU

CAN DO FOR YOUR NEW BABY IS TO HELP

HER GROW UP BEAUTIFUL. AND I

DON'T MEAN BEAUTIFUL IN AN

AFTERSCHOOL SPECIAL KIND OF WAY,

WHEREIN EVERYONE HAS A PERSONAL

BEAUTY THAT RADIATES OUTWARD

FROM THEIR INNER STRENGTH AND

SELF-CONFIDENCE. I'M TALKING

PHYSICAL BEAUTY.

YOU KNOW, REAL BEAUTY.

Conception

Most importantly, be good looking yourself. This will lead
to a good-looking sexual partner, and his handsome sperm
will inevitably meet your sexy egg backstage at an awards show
or in the VIP room of an exclusive club, and they will come
together to make a beautiful fetus.

In the Womb

And I mean a truly beautiful fetus.
Your sonogram is sure to grace the cover of
People's Sexiest Almost People.

Birth

Sashaying down a runway is the only way to give birth to the world's next great supermodel. Your child should be so skinny she slips right out. If not, hold your little whale in there until she gets her weight under control.

Work the Face

Your baby's soft bones are your friend! You can pretty much shape it any way you want. You're going to want to push back and away from the center of the face. Your child is going to be "kitten-in-a-wind-tunnel" sexy in no time!

Diet

Baby fat? Ugh, your child disgusts me. Time to force a tight waistline onto that flabby frame. High-end fashion models subsist on a diet of painkillers, cigarettes, and vodka-waters. If your baby asks to throw a slice of lime in there, you slap it right out of his hand.

Inspiration

Put pictures of really skinny models up all over your child's room and ask them to compare themselves daily. It's humanly impossible to achieve this level of skinniness because it is really a product of all the digital manipulation, so your child will never reach a point where she will be done dieting, and she'll be one step closer to being really good looking.

Friends

It's a fact that gorgeous models only hang out with other gorgeous and/or rich people. The air exhaled by average-looking people is too high in calories to risk being around it. Make sure play dates are only with the beautiful babies in the neighborhood, and always include at least an hour of catwalk crawling, makeup, and champagne.

Prescription Drugs

Not to paint the world with one brush, but all supermodels absolutely love prescription drugs. You can take as many as you want, and as long as a doctor prescribed them, to somebody, you're just doing it for your health.

Birthdays

Having an extravagant birthday is a great way to
reinforce the gorgeous lifestyle and remind everyone
how beautiful your baby really is. On the outside.
Opulent decor, an exclusive guest list, and a celebrity chef.
Hire Rihanna to fight Taylor Swift.

Appropriate Names

FOR A BOY:
Tre Hunkerton
Gerald Jawbone

FOR A GIRL:
Ms. Radiant Cover
Angelica L'Fierce

How to Raise a Pro Athlete

**LIVE THE CAREFREE LIFE OF SPORTS SUPERSTARS
SUCH AS TIGER WOODS AND BRETT FAVRE.**

TRUTH: WE HAVE CHILDREN IN A DESPERATE FINAL ATTEMPT TO ACHIEVE THE GOALS THAT WE OURSELVES FAILED TO REACH IN LIFE. SINCE YOU CAN READ AND ARE NOT PARTYING OR PLAYING SPORTS RIGHT NOW, IT'S OBVIOUS YOU ARE NOT A PRO ATHLETE. YOUR DREAMS FOR SPORTS STARDOM CRASHED LONG AGO, BUT JUNIOR'S KNEES ARE STILL FRESH. NOW STRAP HIM TO THAT TREADMILL, AND LET'S MOLD YOU THE NEXT SPORTS SUPERSTAR.

Conception

Eighty percent of pro athletes are born in the first three months of the year; 100 percent of accountants are born in the final three. Ideally you want your child born on January 1. A day earlier, and they're the runt of their year; a day later, and some other kid has a twenty-four-hour better chance of hoisting the Heisman. March 24 is going to be a big day for you.

In the Womb

Unless you're trying to raise a pro jockey (yeah, right), you're going to have to provide your fetus some serious calories. I'm not talking about your prenatal ginger vitamin shake with lemongrass. If anything, that just knocked ten points off his batting average. You're eating for two now, and one of you is a pro linebacker. It's buffet time.

Delivery

Hold a football out for junior as he passes through the birth canal. If fumbled, repeat until he makes the play. Everyone has to make sacrifices, honey.

Diet

Nothing builds raw strength like cooked meat. Massive chunks of pure cow power transferred directly from the ranch into your future hall of famer. If her breakfast didn't contain the ingredient beefsteak, it better be because you didn't want to spoil her dessert (beefsteak).

Agent

Your child's agent is you. Show your value early by negotiating them a great position in preschool (near the hamster). Collect your 20 percent commission in gold stars.

PRO ATHLETE

Appropriate Names

FOR A GIRL:
Florence Griffith Kournikova
Danica Patrick Andretti

FOR A BOY:
Lion Forrest
Joe Superbowl

How to Raise a Bestselling Author

HAHAHA, WHO ARE YOU ASKING???

No Idea.

How to Raise a Stephen Colbert

TEDDY BALD EAGLES, NOT TEDDY BEARS.

ARE YOU AN INCREDIBLY PATRIOTIC
PARENT WHO IS UNSURE OF WHERE
YOU STAND ON THE ISSUES?
(HINT: OUTRAGED.) ARE YOU
POSITIVE BEARS ARE SOULLESS
KILLING MACHINES WHO ARE ALSO
LETTING MEXICANS ACROSS THE
BORDER TO STEAL AMERICAN JOBS?
IF THIS IS YOU, THEN YOU SHOULD
SERIOUSLY CONSIDER MOLDING YOUR
CHILD INTO STEPHEN COLBERT.

Conception

Four words: Stephen Colbert's Formula 401.
Premium man seed.

In the Womb

Constantly standing at attention and belting out
"The Star Spangled Banner" and "God Bless America"
for every second that you're awake.
And some when you're asleep.

Birth

Legend has it that Stephen was born in a bald eagle's nest on top of Mount Rushmore. So you'll want to go ahead and try to emulate that.

Childhood

After his mandatory three hours of self-affirmation in front of the mirror before bed, tuck your favorite little opinion man in carefully so as not to wrinkle his suit. Wish him sweet dreams and kiss him on the forehead as he snuggles up with his favorite gun, "Sweetness."

Holiday

Every holiday should have a GI Joe theme. Once Stephen is enjoying himself as a "real American hero," smash all his patriotic toys with a teddy bear. Bears are not to be trusted.

Diet

Only let little Stephen eat apple pie made by someone's
grandma who fought in WWII and voted against Clinton.

Appropriate Names

FOR A BOY:
Edwin … hahaha, just kidding,
it's Stephen.

FOR A GIRL:
Stephen

FOR A MEXICAN:
Esteban Colberto

How to Raise a Doctor

GET RICH ... AND LIVE FOREVER.

WITH A DOCTOR IN THE FAMILY,

YOU CAN TAKE THE PROACTIVE STRATEGY

OF MEDICATING LONG BEFORE THE

PROBLEMS EVER ARISE. SWAP IN A DONOR

LIVER BEFORE A BIG NIGHT OF

DRINKING. OXYCONTIN TO FIGHT

ANY POTENTIAL HEADACHES.

WELCOME TO INVINCIBLE.

DOCTOR

Conception

To get inside a doctor's medical genes, you're going to need a lot of appointments. Finally, irritable bowel syndrome is paying off! Try to describe your symptoms in the sexiest possible terms. Intense. Explosive. Sweating. Fiery.

In the Womb

Kick off your child's education with a basic familiarization with the organs surrounding her in the womb. Try a little yogurt with a generous helping of MRI dye. Your throat, stomach, intestines, and bladder will be lit up like a Christmas tree for your fetus MD to study.

Delivery

Presiding as lead physician over her own birth is a great start for your little MD. Her future boss will marvel as she helps her mother with her breathing, turns herself the right side around, and calls out the centimeters dilated.

Childhood

For their first few years make sure he does everything himself, takes orders from everyone, and doesn't get any sleep. Leave a cell phone in your little doctor's crib to get him used to being on call. Remember, a missed call might lead to a malpractice suit. What's a malpractice suit? It's that mean lady from *101 Dalmatians,* just answer the phone!

Toys

You love your child and for that reason they can have any toy in the world. As long as that toy is Operation. Let him know that every time the buzzer goes off someone dies. Like poor Teddy, Elmo, and Mr. Cuddles, all buried in the backyard. For eternity.

Appropriate Names

FOR A GIRL:
Elaine Notthenurse

FOR A BOY:
Doc
Dock
Doke (if you're Russian)

How to Raise a Pageant Queen

THEY JUST DON'T GROW UP FAST ENOUGH.

WHEN YOU THINK OF THE PURE

INNOCENT BEAUTY OF A SMALL CHILD,

IS THERE A TINY PART OF YOU THAT

JUST WANTS TO SMOTHER IT IN LIPSTICK

WHILE BLEACHING ITS HAIR AND FOR

GOD'S SAKE LET'S DO SOMETHING

ABOUT THOSE TEETH!???

THIS CHAPTER MIGHT BE FOR YOU.

Conception

The wonder and joy of being judged should be present in
your child's life from the beginning. The very beginning.
Before you get down to business, have the neighbors over,
the mailman, and that really serious lady from down at the
bank who you know will really tell it like it is.

Remember to smile.

In the Womb

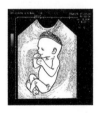

When you have your ultrasound done, give the photos to a
professional fetus artist to touch up digitally. By the time you
show the images to friends and family, your perfectly
made-up baby should be wearing an evening dress,
high heels, and a Miss Uterus sash.

Birth

In the final moments before your child enters this world, take some time to appreciate that swollen and stretch-marked belly. Now write your surrogate a check for her final payment and thank God that didn't happen to you.

Childhood

Skip it.

Routines

A great way to wow the judges is to base your child's routine on your favorite movie. The whore in *Pretty Woman* is an obvious choice, but sadly, it's already been done. Think of other classic kid-friendly characters such as Natalie Portman in *Black Swan* and the stunning Charlize Theron in *Monster*.

Waxing

Just hold her down. The unwanted hair and physical scars will be gone in seconds, while the emotional scars you can't even see.

Diet

Absolutely!

Teen Years

Time to enter the big time, Miss USA, and join the ranks of other successful winners who have given us world peace and ended hunger around the world.
Thanks, ladies!

Adulthood

They grow up so fast! It feels like your baby was just born last month ... and she was! Yet like with Darth Vader, it's difficult to spot any real baby under all that plastic hardware. She didn't even get ID'd at the liquor store last week. It brings a tear to the eye. (A prudent parent will have the tear ducts sealed up to protect eyeliner applications.)

Retirement

When your child turns twelve, she'll most likely sue you for custody of herself, but you remind little Miss Attitude exactly who it was that made her. And you literally made her, out of sculpting clay, ivory, beige paint, the mane of a lion, and a couple of big marbles for eyes. If she wants to leave you at this point, chances are the whole outer structure will hold together without the child inside. Good riddance!

Appropriate Names

Miss
Beauty
Queen

ꙮꙮ

About the Authors

D. HORNBY is so dedicated to molding children
that he had two beautiful twins of his own. He lives on a
small island in British Colulmbia and laughs at people with
plumbing and store bought clothes.

SEAN CAMPBELL is childless, so therefore
his molding skills are innate. He lives in Vancouver,
British Colulmbia, and once tried to learn how to play the
now dusty piano in his house. It mocks him daily.

They've raised your children, now let them solve
all your financial problems with their first book,
How to Survive the Next Recession. Their moms both thought
it was "really nice."

They both write for PseudoExperts.com.
You're welcome.